This book was made especially for

Claire Hobbs

with love from
Grama Judie
12-25-97

Santa's Story

Written by

John B. Hefty

Illustrated by

Lyn Gray Rackley

Page 4 from Clement C. Moore's "A Visit From St. Nicholas"

Printed in USA • Patent Numbers 5,190,316 & 5,454,678
ISBN 1-880453-04-5

'Twas the night before Christmas
and all through the house,
not a creature was stirring,
not even a mouse.

Claire
Buddy

Claire's
Room
Claire

Claire in her nightshirt
settles into bed
with visions of dolls
dancing in her head.

You've heard this before,
this story's not new.
I've added a twist,
your name's in here too.

I'm jolly and round
and I wear a red suit,

I visit Hopkins,
in a sled filled with loot!

To: Quinn
To: Claire

And what is this loot
that I bring in my sled?
Simply toys, like dolls,
and balls that are red.

December

There are clothes and shoes
and candy canes pink,
and then there's some coal
for the naughty kids, I think.

Some say that I'm Santa,
some say I'm a fad,
some folks even say
I look just like your dad.

But one thing's for certain
on this special night,

The world stops its churning
and pushing its might.

The smokestacks
are turned off,
the workers go home,

machines become silent
from Hopkins to Rome.

Up in the sky,
late at night there's a glow,
where a special star twinkled
many years ago.

Peace and goodwill
fill our hearts from the light.
Mary gave birth
to Baby Jesus that night.

The Hobbs'

Wise men brought gifts,
they came from afar,
they found their way there,
they followed the star.

The rest of the story is told in a book
called the Bible, it's great,
one day take a look.

Now onward and upward
I'll sail through the night.
I'm still the tradition
of what's good and what's right.

And because you'll get presents,
I know Christmas day
will not be forgotten
as you laugh and you play.
But remember the reason
for peace and great joy,
it comes from our Christ,
and not just from a toy.

To: Claire
To: Claire

So hang your stockings
by the chimney with care,
don't worry about me,
I'll still be there.

I'll munch on the snacks,
drink the milk that you leave,
I do it each year
the same time, Christmas Eve.

My reindeer are ready
the time is just right.
Go to sleep now, Claire,
Merry Christmas,
Good Night!

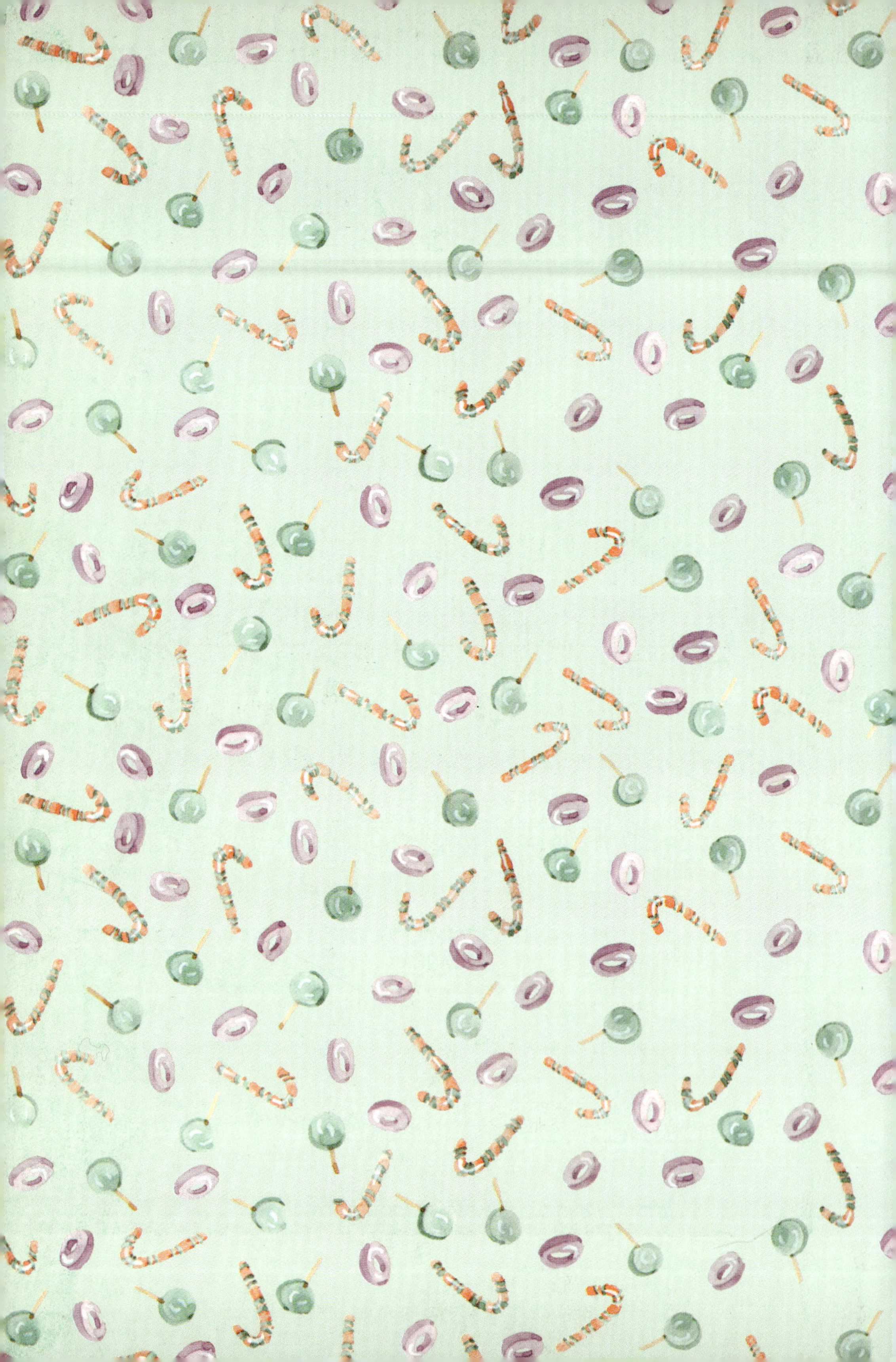